STEP INTO THE WORLD OF
ANCIENT
CHINA

CONTENTS

CONTENTS

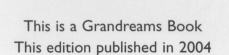

This is a Grandreams Book
This edition published in 2004

Grandreams Books Ltd
4 North Parade, Bath BA1 1LF, UK

Designed and packaged by
Q2A Design Studio

Printed in China

EMPERORS AND DYNASTIES

Ancient China is the oldest continuous civilization in the world. It flourished for thousands of years, until 1911 A.D. The earliest people in China were farmers who settled in villages and towns along the fertile Yellow River.

Gradually, the small settlements were divided into different states. Then Shi Huangdi (259-210 B.C.), the king of the powerful state of Qin, overthrew the others to become the first emperor of China.

The First Emperor

Under Emperor Shi Huangdi, the Chinese empire was expanded to include a capital city, roads and huge palaces and forts. He also introduced new laws, a system of writing and an official currency. However, Shi Huangdi was known to be an unkind emperor. He would kill or banish anyone who went against his wishes. It is said that he was brutal enough to bury his rivals alive!

Diverse Dynasties

Ancient China was ruled by many different families of emperors and empresses. The period under a particular family of rulers was called a dynasty. After Shi Huangdi died, his Qin dynasty came to an end, marking the beginning of a new one.

Shi Huangdi is also remembered because he began the construction of the Great Wall of China

EMPERORS AND DYNASTIES

 Along which two rivers did Chinese civilization begin?

The civilization of China began along the Huang He (Yellow River) and the Chang Jiang (Long River).

Warriors in ancient China were known to be extremely brave, strong and well-trained in combat

 Who protected China and its emperors from enemies?

It was the job of the ancient Chinese military to protect their rulers and the province. Warriors in ancient China were strong and armed with weapons like bows, arrows and spears. They dressed in decorative silk uniforms that were embroidered with images of dragons and birds.

Confucius was one of the most influential figures in the history of China and the world

 Was Confucius (551-479 B.C.) an emperor?

Confucius was the first and most famous professional teacher in ancient China. Sometimes, he also acted as a political advisor to emperors. Confucius opened the first school for the common people. His teachings went onto to have a lasting influence on the Chinese way of life.

 How many dynasties were there in ancient China?

The world's oldest continuous civilization has been ruled by numerous dynasties. However, the main families that ruled ancient China, from the 21st century BC to 1000 A.D., included the Xia, Shang, Zhou, Qin, Han, Sui and Tang dynasties.

What was the Silk Road?

 The Silk Road is the name of an ancient trading route from China to the Mediterranean Sea. The road was named after the silk products that were taken along it. Gradually, many more trading goods were transported along the Silk Road.

How did China get its name?

 China is so called after its first dynasty – the Qin Dynasty, which is pronounced as 'chin'.

How did emperors travel from place to place?

 Emperors and other important people in ancient China travelled in palanquins or sedan chairs. There were different carrying chairs for different occasions. The most common was the casual litter, which the emperor used around his palace.

The emperor used his casual litter for day-to-day travel from place to place

■ It is thought that ancient Chinese emperors regularly ate mushrooms, which became known as 'the food of emperors'.

■ In ancient China, it was customary to bury an empress separately from her husband.

■ Axes, knives and other weapons made of either bronze or iron were commonly used by the ancient Chinese military. These were also sometimes used as tools for farming activities.

Hand axes like this one began to be used in China as early as 8000 years ago

What kind of luxuries did Emperor Hu enjoy?

It has been said that for his hunting trips, Emperor Hu (Hu the Tiger) had a litter with a revolving coach, so that he could turn in any direction and shoot! It seems he was so heavy that about 20 men had to carry him! Legend has it that Hu the Tiger also had a 500-member, all-girl orchestra, battalions of female soldiers and a bathhouse, air-conditioned by a system of running water.

What was the jian?

The jian was one of the most common weapons used in ancient China. A straight, double-edged sword, it was also regarded as a sacred weapon. During the Spring and Autumn and Warring States periods, high quality bronze jians became popular.

The jian sword was used by warriors mainly for self defence

 Did emperors in ancient China keep any pets?

Research has revealed that ancient Chinese emperors kept giant pandas for pets! It was believed that pandas could ward off evil spirits and natural disasters. The Giant Panda was called Daxiongmao, which means 'great bear cat' in Chinese.

The Chinese have practiced fortune-telling for thousands of years

 How did fortune-tellers in ancient China help emperors?

The ancient Chinese made great advances in the field of astrology. They had many different ways of predicting the future. Emperors had special court astrologers and fortune-tellers who made predictions relating to the country and its government.

天文學家

 Who were the 'sons of heaven'?

Emperors in ancient China considered themselves to be the 'sons of heaven'. The Mandate of Heaven, an ancient Chinese belief, gave them the right to rule.

RELIGIONS AND BELIEFS

In ancient China, religion was an important part of everyday life. Many different belief systems influenced the ancient Chinese during their civilization.

In the Beginning

At first, the people of ancient China believed in deities of nature. Later, the people only worshipped the all-important God of Heaven, Shang-Ti.

Buddhism, Taoism and Confucianism

Chinese religion has been shaped by three philosophies – Buddhism, Taoism and Confucianism. Buddhism stated that people had to free themselves of desire in order to be happy. Taoism maintained that people in China were only a small part of the natural universe and that they must fit into it instead of trying to change it. Confucianism taught people to follow ancestral customs and duties to live peacefully.

Gods & Goddesses

With the emergence of new religious beliefs, the ancient Chinese began to worship a variety of gods and goddesses like Ba Xian (Eight Immortals) and Guanyin, the Goddess of Mercy.

The ancient Chinese Goddess of Mercy is also known as Kuan Yin, Quan'Am, Kannon and Kanin

RELIGIONS AND BELIEFS

 What were the 'Three Teachings'?

Buddhism, Taoism and Confucianism made up the 'Three Teachings', the main systems of belief in ancient China. Also known as the 'Three Doctrines', the religions flourished in ancient China during the second and third centuries.

Who were the teachers of the 'Three Doctrines'?

Buddhism, Taoism and Confucianism were taught by three different preachers. Confucius founded the philosophy of Confucianism and Laozi preached Taoism. Siddhartha Gautam (Lord Buddha) was the founder of Buddhism, China's most popular religion.

The Indian religion of Buddhism was introduced to the Chinese in the first century and its influence had spread to the whole of China by 384 A.D.

The round and happy Laughing Buddha is considered to be one of the Gods of Wealth in China

 What is the significance of the Laughing Buddha?

Buddhism in ancient China is associated with the popular folk figure of the Laughing Buddha. Also known as the Maitreya Buddha ('The Kindly One'), the figure of a happy and pot-bellied monk symbolises a prosperous future, generosity and happiness.

What did the ancient Chinese believe about solar and lunar eclipses?

The ancient Chinese though that solar eclipses occurred when a dragon tried to swallow the Sun! Similarly, they believed that lunar eclipses meant that the moon was being eaten.

What kind of ritual object was used in ancient Buddhist temples?

Kongo bells with prongs and jewelled handles were used during religious training in ancient China. Practitioners would ring these bells at the beginning of a ritual to call Buddha. The bells would also be sounded at the end of the ritual to send him back. Five-pronged Kongo bells were the most commonly used type of bell for this ritual.

An ancient Chinese Kongo bell

Which mythological creature has been associated with China since ancient times?

The dragon has been associated with China since ancient times. In ancient China, the dragon represented joy, immortality and fertility. Dragons were also believed to drive away evil spirits.

How, according to ancient Chinese belief, were clouds and storms created?

People in ancient China believed that clouds were actually the breath of a sleeping dragon. If the dragon smoked while in bed, the cloud became stormy and lightning would appear if the dragon was woken up before his eight hours of sleep!

FACT BOX

■ The ancient Chinese believed that odd numbers were masculine and even numbers were feminine! That is why the number 9, the largest single digit, stood for ultimate masculinity. Therefore, number 9 represented the greatest sovereignty of the emperor.

■ People in ancient China believed that the heart was the centre of intelligence and the stomach was the seat of power.

■ An important ancient Chinese belief held that the universe was created with two kinds of energies – yin and yang. The ancient Chinese believed that these two opposite yet balanced energies were responsible for any change or movement in the universe.

The iconic yin-yang sign of China is also known as the Tai-Chi symbol

RELIGIONS AND BELIEFS

What were spirit beasts and guardians?

Statues of mythical beasts were made to guard ancient Chinese tombs. Guardian beasts were often in the form of half-man and half-beast. They were said to scare away evil spirits and tomb robbers.

Which creature were pearls believed to originate from?

The ancient Chinese believed that pearls were created inside the brains of dragons!

An unusual spirit beast from the Tang dynasty of ancient China

Which animal was regarded as lucky in ancient China?

In ancient China, the pig represented good luck and fortune. It was believed that anyone who owned a pig would live and eat well.

Ritual discs played an important and spiritual role in ancient Chinese burial practice

What did the turtle represent to the ancient Chinese?

The people of ancient China saw the turtle as a symbol of peace and long life.

What were bi discs?

Bi discs were round ritual objects with a hole in the middle. They were probably placed on the jade suits of dead bodies. The first known bi discs, which date back to Neolithic China, were not as decorative as their later counterparts. It is thought that bi discs symbolised the sun and helped the soul of the dead travel peacefully to heaven.

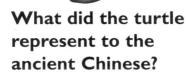

TOMBS AND BURIALS

The ancient Chinese, like the Egyptians, believed in afterlife and mummification. However, their methods of preserving and burying dead bodies were quite different.

Tombs and Mummies

The ancient Chinese believed that people travelled to another life after they died. As such, the bodies of the dead were preserved and buried in pyramid-like tombs. The earliest Chinese tombs were made of wood or stone.

The emperors and nobles of ancient China were buried in elaborate tombs. Precious artefacts, daily utensils and pottery figures of animals and servants were buried with the body.

Spirit Guardians

Royal tombs were usually situated at the end of a pathway known as the 'spirit path'. This road was guarded by statues of warriors, sacred animals and mythical creatures. Often, colourful Buddhist figures called *lokapalas* meaning 'worldly guardian' were placed inside the tombs to protect the body.

In ancient China, lokapalas were considered to be the guardians of earth's four cardinal directions

13

TOMBS AND BURIALS

How do we know that the ancient Chinese believed in life after death?

The discovery of ancient Chinese mummies and tomb-remains tells us about Chinese burial customs. Excavations have revealed that there was a strong belief in life after death.

What did the earliest tombs in ancient China look like?

The earliest tombs in ancient China were in the form of big earthen mounds. They were built above the ground, unlike the later royal tombs, which were underground.

China's earliest tombs were built on ground and were made out of earth

Why were ancient Chinese mummies covered with jade stone?

Mummies in ancient China were cased in a suit of jade. This is because the ancient Chinese believed that jade stone had magical properties and would keep the body from decaying. It was also said to ward off evil spirits.

Which Chinese prince's mummy suit was made of nearly 3000 pieces of jade stone?

Prince Liu Sheng's (154-113 B.C.) suit was made of 2,498 bits of jade. The pieces were stitched with gold wire. It is said that the suit took about 10 years to complete! Prince Liu Sheng's jade casing proved that jade did not have preserving properties, as only some of the prince's teeth remained!

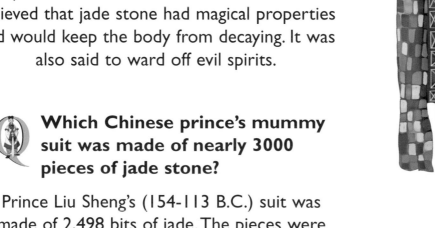

Jade burial suits were usually stitched together with gold wire or threads of silk

Were only models placed inside ancient Chinese tombs?

Before emperors had clay models made for their tombs, actual people and animals were killed and buried to serve their master in the afterlife! This practice of human sacrifice for tomb burial was common until the Qin Dynasty.

The Terracotta Army: the eighth wonder of the world

Which ancient Chinese tomb discovery is sometimes referred to as the Eighth Wonder of the World?

In 1974, around 7,000, life-sized terracotta warriors were accidentally found buried in the city of Xi'an. The discovery led to excavations, which revealed the tomb of Emperor Shi Huangdi. The Underground Terracotta Army was placed in the tomb to protect the emperor and his riches in the afterlife!

Why were models of court entertainers found in ancient Chinese tombs?

Clay models of dancers and musicians were found in numerous ancient Chinese tombs. They were believed to have served as entertainers for the dead person in his or her next life.

■ Among the most important finds from Shang tombs are 'oracle bones', recording the questions that Shang kings wrote to their ancestors. These writings provide important information about the emperors, such as the kind of gods and goddesses they worshipped.

■ The tomb of Marquis Yi housed the emperor's personal gold treasures. Amongst these, a bowl and ladle set is said to be the biggest of its kind from the pre-Qin dynasty.

Amongst the five gold artefacts found in the tomb of Marquis Qi was this elegant gold bowl and ladle set

■ One of the most common tomb guardians in ancient China was the chimera. A chimera was a mythical creature with wings of a bird, the body and face of a lion and the horns of a ram.

TOMBS AND BURIALS

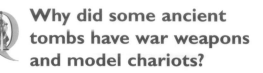

Why did some ancient tombs have war weapons and model chariots?

Weapons and chariots were major symbols of a ruler's military power. During the Shang Dynasty, many tombs were furnished with two-wheeled, horse-drawn chariots.

Coffins in ancient China were often elaborately painted in sacred colours like red

What kind of coffins were made for ancient Chinese emperors?

Tomb coffins in ancient China varied from dynasty to dynasty. They were made of materials such as stone, wood and lacquer. They were often intricately carved with sacred symbols and designs. The colour red was widely used on these coffins, as the ancient Chinese considered it to be auspicious.

Which was the only ancient Chinese tomb not to be found robbed?

The tomb of Fu Hao (a member of the Shang royal family) is the only royal tomb to have been discovered intact. Beneath the dead body, a pit containing the corpses of six dogs was found. The tomb also housed several utensils and artefacts.

Shedding light on a new world: lamps placed inside an ancient Chinese tomb meant to serve as a guiding light for the soul

What were ancient Chinese ritual vessels known as?

Ritual vessels and bells that were placed inside tombs were known as *mingqi*, meaning 'spirit goods'. From the late Zhou Dynasty onwards, people began to make cheap clay replicas of these vessels, since they were rare and costly.

Why were lamps buried along with dead bodies in ancient Chinese tombs?

Lamps made of bronze, silver, celadon and other materials represented the light that was shed upon the dark world within the tomb chamber. These lamps were often crafted in the shape of humans and animals.

CUSTOMS AND FESTIVALS

Celebrations and festivities were an important part of life in ancient China. From religious rituals to cultural customs, there were many occasions to be merry.

New Year's Day

Also called the Spring Festival, the Chinese New Year is determined by the moon's phases. On this day, the Chinese wear new clothes and ask for the blessings of their elders. Firecrackers are burst to ward off evil spirits and grand feasts are held.

For people in ancient China, the events of the New Year determined the events of the entire year. So, on that day, children were told not to cry and adults were not allowed to scold children. Sweeping the floor and washing one's hair was considered unlucky – this was seen as sweeping or washing away one's good fortune!

Dancing Dragons

A trademark of the Chinese is their dragon dance. New Year parades have always included a chain of people disguised as a colourful dragon, dancing on the streets.

According to popular belief, the longer the dragon the more luck he would bring

CUSTOMS AND FESTIVALS

What is the story behind the Dragon Boat Festival?

The Dragon Boat Festival originated in ancient China, to honour Qu Yuan, a patriotic poet in 277 B.C. According to legend, when Qu Yuan heard about his state's defeat in the war, he drowned himself. Hearing about his death, people rushed to the spot to search for his body, but in vain. They threw bamboo leaves stuffed with rice into the water, hoping that the fish would eat the rice instead of the poet!

Why was it considered important to match the birthdays of two people before they could get married?

The custom of birthday matching was considered essential for an auspicious marriage. It was believed that if the birth dates and timings of the woman and man did not match, their marriage would prove disastrous for both the families.

The footbinding custom was practiced in China for nearly 1000 years. It was banned only in 1911, during the reign of China's last dynasty

Which ancient Chinese custom involved the use of lotus shoes?

In ancient China, only women with small feet were considered to be beautiful and of a higher social class. This prompted the custom of foot binding, in which the feet of infant girls were bandaged and bound in shoes called lotus shoes. This cruel custom prevented the feet from growing normally and deformed them.

What is the significance of the ancient Chinese custom of bowing?

Children in ancient China were expected to bow in front of their elders as a sign of respect. Confucius preached that all people should respect and honour their family members.

Bowing in China is still done as a sign of respect or as a gesture of thanks

What were the Three Letters and Six Etiquettes in ancient Chinese marriage?

In ancient China, the customs of Three Letters and Six Etiquettes were essential to marriage. Three letters (Betrothal Letter, Gift Letter and Wedding Letter) formalised the engagement, gifting ceremony and marriage vows. The Six Etiquettes were proposing, birthday matching, engagement gift presentations, wedding gift presentations, choosing the wedding date and finally, the ceremony itself.

In ancient China, huge processions were sent to the bride's house to present her family with gifts

How was the wedding gift presentation ceremony in ancient China performed?

The family of the bridegroom sent a grand procession carrying wedding gifts to the bride and her family. The gifts included tea, lotus seeds, beans, fruits, cakes, coconuts, wine and a moneybox.

The traditional Chinese lantern is a symbol of joy, festivity and luck. Lanterns of all different sizes, shapes and colours are hung during any festive occasion in China even today

What kind of wine was often used in the ceremonies and rituals of ancient China?

Rice wine was an important part of ancient Chinese ceremonies and ritual sacrifices. In 2003, archaeologists unearthed jars of rice wine from an ancient tomb in Xi'an. The tomb dates back to the Western Han dynasty.

FACT BOX

■ Ancient Chinese doctors were paid only if their patients stayed healthy. If a particular doctor's patient kept falling sick, then he had to pay his patient. It is said that if the patient died, a lantern was hung outside the doctor's house!

■ Emperor Mingdi of the Han Dynasty believed that Buddha could dispel darkness. Hence he ordered his people to display lighted lanterns as a symbol of a bright future during what became the Lantern Festival. Celebrated on the first full moon day of the year, it also marks the end of the Chinese New Year.

■ In ancient China, the Feast of Hungry Ghosts was held to honour those dead people who were uncared for in their lifetime. The festival was held during a lunar month when spirits were believed to roam on earth.

CUSTOMS AND FESTIVALS

An ancient Chinese unity jar

During which festival do people give each other red envelopes containing money?

During the Chinese New Year, people give one another red envelopes containing 'lucky money'. The custom is related to the concept of bringing in prosperity and wealth in the year ahead. This custom exists even today.

When were marriage customs in ancient China first systematised?

Chinese marriage customs were first formalised during the Warring States period (402-221 B.C.).

The ancient Chinese held a sacrifice ceremony for their ancestors at midnight

What kind of drinking vessel in ancient China symbolised friendship, love and unity?

Unity jars were used for drinking wine in ancient China. These were so called because they were two jars joined together in the middle as one. Two people, each holding one side of the jar, would drink from it. This represented the strengthening of love, friendship and unity.

How did the ancient Chinese pay respect to their ancestors on New Year's Eve?

Since ancient times, the Chinese stayed at home on New Year's Eve for the Ancestor's Memorial Ceremony. They burned candles and kneeled in front of statues of their ancestors, paying respect and asking for their blessings for the coming year.

Is there a special ancient Chinese festival for cleaning tombs?

One day of the year in China is dedicated for the Tomb Sweeping Festival. Dating back to ancient China, this ritual involves the cleaning of ancestral tombs, as a sign of ancestor worship and respect.

DAILY LIFE

Life in ancient China for most was rural, simple and traditional. But generally, daily activities in ancient China were not very different from activities in today's world.

Hierarchy at Home

The family in ancient China was all-important. It functioned in a strict hierarchy. The father was the ultimate authority and his children had to respect and obey his instructions. Every member of a family had well-defined roles to perform, so as to contribute to the well-being of the family and uphold its reputation.

Working Women

Ancient Chinese women were primarily restricted to the home. Women from peasant families spent their time cooking and cleaning, as well as caring for her children and the elders in the family. Women belonging to royal and noble homes had servants to do the daily chores. Hence they could afford to dress themselves in expensive silks and spend most of their day playing with their children.

Women in ancient China worked at home and their chores included cooking, cleaning, weaving and rearing silkworms

DAILY LIFE

What was Chinese society like?

People in ancient China belonged to one of two broad social classes—the rich or the poor. The rich classes included people of royalty and scholars. Peasants and farmers belonged to the poor category. Emperors lived in large palaces or pagodas. The homes of the rich were situated at one end of the city, while the poor lived at the other end.

Was the traditional Chinese family big in size?

The traditional family in ancient China had many members. Grandparents, parents and children lived together, as this was considered to symbolize good fortune.

What was the main occupation of the ancient Chinese people?

In ancient China, most people were farmers who worked on small plots of land. They lived on the fertile banks of the Yellow River. All members of a family contributed to the process of growing and harvesting crops like wheat, soybeans, barley and rice.

How did farmers in ancient China sell their goods?

Every village and city in ancient China had a marketplace where the farmers could sell their goods or buy whatever they needed.

Ancient China was home to several busy markets, where traders brought and displayed goods such as fruits, vegetables, fabrics, medicines and daily utensils

The ancient Chinese started using oxen for ploughing fields sometime in 1100 B.C.

FACT BOX

 How did ancient Chinese farmers cultivate farm land?

Farmers in ancient China used ox-drawn ploughs to work the soil on their land. Using oxen for pulling the plough became common during the Han Dynasty.

 Which crops were considered most important in ancient China?

The ancient Chinese had five sacred local crops. These were rice, soybeans, wheat, millet and barley. These crops were regarded as healthy and therapeutic.

 How did the ancient Chinese grind rice and flour?

People in ancient China had stone mills for grinding crops like rice and wheat. Flour milling in ancient China was also introduced during the Han Dynasty.

An ancient Chinese miller grinding grains in a hand-operated mill

■ Both men and women in ancient China had long hair. They knotted their hair on top of their heads. Wealthy women spent more time on trying out new hairstyles and decorating their hair with jewels.

■ Women in ancient China used hairpins made of animal bone or precious metals to pin up their knots. Many such hairpins have been unearthed from ancient Chinese tombs.

Early Chinese hairpins made of animal bone

■ In early China, only children of wealthy families could afford to go to school or have private tuitions. Boys were taught academic subjects, while most girls were trained in stitching, cooking and handicrafts.

23

DAILY LIFE

How were tea leaves dried in ancient China?

The ancient Chinese picked the tea leaves and laid them out under the sun. The leaves were then hand-turned and finally, they were dried out over a fire.

What kind of coins were used in ancient China?

Coins in ancient China were in the shape of spades, knives, shells, bridges and weapons! Round coins came into use later.

China was the first country to use coins and paper money

What was the dragon-backbone machine?

A chain pump known as the dragon-backbone machine was used by farmers in ancient China to raise water. The machine helped peasants to water the rice fields.

What kind of clothes did people in ancient China wear?

Poor men in ancient China wore baggy trousers and shirts, while poor women dressed in ordinary robes or dresses. They had shoes made of woven straw. The rich on the other hand could afford to wear clothes and shoes made of silk.

What kind of homes did people live in during pre-historic China?

The earliest inhabitants of ancient China lived in simple huts set close together in farming villages. The huts were either pyramid-shaped or circular and made of straw and clay.

The village huts of ancient China were often called beehive huts because of their shape

ARTS AND CRAFTS

Home to a variety of unique art and craft forms, ancient China was a major hub of creativity. From the simple earthen pots of to the artistic use of jade, the ancient Chinese were skilled artisans.

The Best of Bronze

The ancient Chinese are credited with the invention of bronze. They made tools and artefacts out of it. Highly skilled craftsmen sculpted bronze statues for tomb entrances and royal palaces. Daily utensils were also often bronze, carved with figures of dragons and other sacred Chinese symbols.

Calligraphy Culture

Chinese calligraphy is roughly 4000 years old. According to legend, a man named Gang Xie invented the Chinese language and calligraphy evolved soon after. The ancient art of brush calligraphy involved the painting of different Chinese characters with fine strokes of bamboo brushes made of wolf hair.

Chinese calligraphers had to memorise about 40,000 characters, which took them years of study!

How did the ancient Chinese make silk?

Silk production in ancient China involved collecting silkworms from mulberry trees. The worms were fed until they formed a cocoon. These were then placed in boiling water, where the cocoons opened up into single threads of silk. These threads were reeled and finally woven into silk fabric.

The Chinese kept their silk production technique a secret for about 2000 years

What were known as the three 'perfections' in ancient China?

In ancient China, poetry, calligraphy and painting represented the three 'perfections'. All educated people were required to learn them.

Chinese embroidery is said to be the oldest known form of embroidery in the world

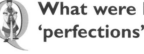

Which was the earliest evidence of ancient Chinese art?

The first known evidence of art in ancient China was pottery decorated with geometric patterns. Pottery was the most common artwork in Neolithic China. Storage jars and bowls were richly decorated with geometrical shapes and swirling designs in colours like red and black.

Did the ancient Chinese practice embroidery?

Embroidery was an important form of art in ancient China. Both silk and embroidered products were important exports for the traders. One of the early techniques was hand embroidery with coloured threads, on fabrics that were stretched tightly across a wooden frame.

How skilled were painters in ancient China?

Artisans in ancient China were very skilled painters. This is evident from their handiwork on tomb wall murals, silk scroll paintings and pottery. Landscape watercolour paintings on silk scrolls has remained a Chinese speciality.

A typical ancient Chinese scroll painting

What kinds of materials were used to make jewellery in ancient China?

Necklaces, earrings and bracelets were made from materials like gold, silver, jade, coloured glass, ivory, marble, crystal and other precious stones.

Did the ancient Chinese invent lacquer, porcelain and bronze art?

Porcelain, bronze and lacquer were all invented in ancient China. Celadon was the most common form of Chinese porcelain, while the tri-colour glazed Sancai ceramics became popular in the Tang dynasty.

■ According to legend, ancient Chinese artists never painted the feet of women. The reason for this is not known.

■ The horse was a regular feature of ancient Chinese art. Artists would often paint images of galloping horses to symbolise power and movement. Craftsmen also made bronze and stone sculptures of the animal for tomb and palace entrances.

■ Multicoloured glass beads were amongst the earliest examples of glass in ancient China. They have been found in tombs dating back to the Bronze Age, suggesting that by the fifth century B.C., glass artefacts were being crafted in China.

Glass beads in ancient China were used in the making of clothes and jewellery

ARTS AND CRAFTS

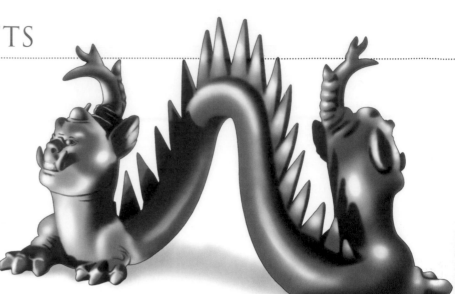

How many different types of jade stone did the ancient Chinese use in their art?

Green jade was the most valuable stone in ancient China. However, white, red and yellow jade was also used by artists and craftsmen.

The sacred double-headed serpent represents Goddess Nuwa and God Fuxi, the creators of humanity according to ancient Chinese mythology

Which ancient Chinese invention made possible the mass production of brocade?

The invention of a draw loom in the second century A.D. allowed Chinese craftsmen to produce brocade on a large scale.

Which pre-historic deities of ancient China were depicted as a double-headed serpent?

Nuwa and Fuxi were often depicted together as a double-headed serpent. Intricately carved sculptures of this mythological figure have been found in some tombs.

What were erdang?

Erdang were special earrings worn by women in ancient China more than 2,500 years ago. These were often buried along with the dead bodies of their owners. The earliest known erdang was found in a tomb of the Spring and Autumn Period (770-476 B.C.).

Chinese celadon pottery is characterised by a pale green glaze. It was first produced in the city of Longquan during the Jin Dynasty (265-376 B.C.)

What is celadon?

Celadon is a type of glazed potteryware that is believed to have been invented in China over 2,000 years ago. It has often been referred to as the most difficult style of pottery to master.

ARCHITECTURE

Architecture in ancient China has a colourful history. From simple huts and courtyard houses to elaborate palaces and temples, ancient Chinese builders left behind a unique style of architecture.

The Art of Architecture

Ancient Chinese architecture has often been compared to the traditional art of calligraphy. The typical curved and symmetrical roofs of the buildings and monuments have a striking likeness to the artistic brush strokes of Chinese writers and artists. Curved lines, squares and spheres were considered sacred and lucky.

Pretty Pavilions

The pavilion, also known as ting in Chinese, was made of wood, bamboo or stone. They were built symmetrically, with curved roof edges and designed in shapes like squares, triangles, octagons and five-petal flowers. Some pavilions were built near lakes to create a reflection of the pavilion in the water.

The roofs of ancient Chinese pavilions were supported by columns instead of walls

ARCHITECTURE

What is Feng Shui?

Feng Shui (pronounced as fung shway) is an ancient Chinese belief that all objects should be in harmony with their surroundings. The principles of Feng Shui are applied even in modern times, with furniture and decorations being arranged in harmony within a building.

Why is the Great Wall of China considered to be an architectural marvel?

The Great Wall of China is the world's longest man-made structure. Over 4,000 miles in length, the Great Wall was made entirely by hand. Shi Huangdi had it built as a defensive wall to protect China from its enemies. It is said that the emperor used around 300,000 workers for this purpose. The first part of the Wall took 10 years to complete. It continued to be expanded during the rule of later dynasties.

What kind of motifs and elements are considered to be auspicious in Feng Shui?

Feng Shui encourages elements such as wind chimes, water fountains, crystals, candles, incense and brass ornaments.

Why was the colour yellow used in ancient Chinese palaces?

Yellow was considered to represent the earth. The ancient Chinese believed that yellow was the essence of all things. Only emperors had the right to associate themselves with the colour!

The length of the Great Wall of China is believed to equal the distance between Miami City in the U.S. and the North Pole!

Which are the oldest stone structures in China?

The Big Buddha: the famous statue at the Yungang Caves

The Yungang Caves near the city of Datong are the oldest stone structures in China. They date back to the Northern Wei Dynasty. A total of 53 caves contain more than 50,000 religious statues. The fifth cave holds the largest Buddha sculpture of the Caves.

What did tombs in ancient China look like?

The structure and design of ancient Chinese tombs changed with the dynasties and customs. During the Han Dynasty, for instance, tombs had many chambers, while Shang tombs were in the form of a single pit. The tomb of Marquis Yi of the Warring States Period (475-221 B.C.) was created to resemble the layout of his palace.

What kind of materials were used to construct tombs in ancient China?

Tombs in ancient China were made using stone or clay tiles. These tiles were often painted or carved with images from daily life or symbols that were thought to help the soul travel to the afterlife. Some tiles had relief sculptures of animals like the ram, dragon and horse.

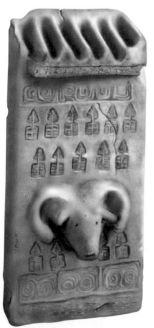

An ancient Chinese tomb tile decorated with the head of a ram

ARCHITECTURE

 Which architectural element in ancient China was said to refresh the spirit?

The ancient Chinese believed water gardens refreshed the spirits of people and drove away stress.

A relief carving of the Chinese dragon

 Is there a Leaning Tower of China?

The Tiger Hill Pagoda (Yunyan Temple Pagoda) in Suzhou, is often referred to as the Leaning Tower of China. It is so called because it started to lean in 1638 A.D. It was first built in the Sui Dynasty (581-618 A.D.).

What were the two main motifs used for decorating palaces and temples?

Dragons and phoenixes have always been the main motifs of decoration in Chinese architecture. Both beasts were seen as sacred guardian gods. Imagery of the dragon in Chinese architecture dates back to ancient tomb paintings and carvings.

Why is the Qianxun Pagoda unique?

Qianxun Pagoda is one of the most well-known architectural landmarks of ancient China. Built sometime in the Tang Dynasty, the square-shaped pagoda is the biggest of the three Pagodas of Dali. Its unique feature is that it has sixteen-tier eaves, which was rare in ancient Chinese pagodas.

What name was given to the residences of important people in ancient China?

The ancient Chinese referred to palaces, temples and certain houses as 'gongs'. During the Qin dynasty, the term was used to describe a group of buildings in which emperors lived and worked. Gradually, all living spaces of an emperor were called gongs.

The Qianxun Pagoda was built sometime in the ninth century B.C. and is around 70 m (230 feet) tall

GAMES AND ENTERTAINMENT

The ancient Chinese spent much of their free time on art, music and theatre.

Let the Music Play!

Music was central to the lives of most people in ancient China. The emperor's court had special musicians and dancers to entertain him and his guests. Poor people also played a wide range of instruments, such as stone chimes, bronze bells, drums and bamboo flutes. Bamboo flutes discovered inside an ancient Chinese tomb a few years ago, were declared to be the oldest instruments in the world. The pipa, a traditional Chinese instrument, was especially popular at court banquets and feasts.

Fun in the Outdoors

Games and other outdoor activities were also very popular in ancient China. Emperors and nobles often went hunting and watched horse races. Other forms of entertainment included gambling, watching juggling performances or playing card games. Outdoor sports resembling badminton, football, baseball and tennis were also played. Many others liked indoor games. These included a tile game called mahjong, dominoes and Chinese checkers. Children often played with puzzles, masks and toys made of clay.

The four-stringed pipa is one of the oldest musical instruments of China

 How did the ancient Chinese entertain themselves in their free time?

The ancient Chinese played indoor and outdoor games during their leisure time. They also watched operas, plays and martial art combats. Children played in the courtyards with toys and their pets.

Ancient Chinese children at play

 How was *Liubo* played?

The popular ancient Chinese game of *Liubo* was played by 2-4 people who shook bamboo sticks or dice to move pieces around a board. Very little is known about the rules and objectives of the game. However, it is believed that *Xiangqi*, the Chinese version of chess, was derived from this game. *Liubo* was popular in China from the sixth century B.C. until sometime in the 12th century A.D.

Bells in ancient China were also symbols of status and power

 Which was the earliest type of musical bell in ancient China?

The *taozhong* was the first kind of bell used in ancient China. The instrument was played by labourers in their leisure time.

 Which ancient Chinese bells sounded two different musical notes?

Zhong bells, which were sounded by striking, could produce two different notes because of their unique shape. They were oval-shaped and looked somewhat like tiles.

 Why were bells such important instruments in ancient China?

Ancient Chinese bells became important with the advent of Buddhism and Buddhist temples in China. Rounded bells replaced the earlier, tile-like bells.

Which ancient Chinese toy is compared to the rotors of a helicopter?

The *taketonbo*, or 'bamboo dragonfly', was an ancient Chinese flying toy dating back to 400 A.D. The toy had a propeller-like blade attached to a bamboo stick with a chord (string) around it. The toy was released into the air by pulling the chord. The *taketonbo* could fly on its own for some time!

The propeller-like Chinese bamboo dragonfly is considered to be one of the earliest 'flying machines'

How did musicians in ancient China play their instruments?

Musicians in ancient China were very skilled. It is believed that some musicians played as many as three instruments at a time, using their hands, feet and mouth!

The ancient Chinese musician: master of all instruments!

FACT BOX

■ The kite was invented in ancient China. People spent a lot of time flying kites made of silk and paper. It is thought that kites were also used by the Chinese military to scare off their enemies!

■ *Liubo* included the use of dice that had 18 sides. They were often used instead of bamboo sticks. The counters on the *Liubo* board were moved according to readings from these dice.

An 18-sided dice used in the ancient Chinese game of liubo

■ Ancient tomb paintings reveal that polo was a popular sport in China. The wealthy and important people held polo matches and played in them. The game flourished even more after the Chinese invented the horse stirrup.

GAMES AND ENTERTAINMENT

Was the yo-yo invented by the ancient Chinese?

The yo-yo is said to be derived from the *diabolo*. The *diabolo* was an ancient Chinese spinning game, using a hollow toy that was tied to strings and manipulated by the hands to spin. Unlike yo-yos, *diabolos* were not permanently fixed to strings. When spun very quickly, they made a humming sound.

Where is the single largest collection of ancient musical instruments?

The single largest collection of musical instruments from an ancient culture was discovered in the tomb of Marquis Yi, an ancient Chinese emperor.

The Chinese diabolo is regarded as an ancestor of the yo-yo

What was *pai gow*?

Pai gow was a betting game played in ancient China. It was played with Chinese dominoes or tiles.

Tai chi: The national form of exercise in ancient China

Did football originate in ancient China?

The ancient Chinese were known to play the earliest form of football, known as *Tsu Chu*. It was played during 255-206 B.C. and involved the kicking of a leather ball with the feet. In fact, the word literally means 'kicking the ball with feet'! *Tsu Chu* was also used for training soldiers.

What kind of marital arts were practiced in ancient China?

Martial art forms like *tai chi* and *kung fu* originated in ancient China. *Tai chi* is characterised by gentle stretches and body movements, performed at a slow pace. Also known as shadow boxing, *tai chi* was believed to have positive effects on the body and mind.

ANCIENT CHINESE CUISINE

Dumplings, chopsuey, chow mein and jasmine tea – when we think of the Chinese, one of the things that immediately comes to mind is their traditional and colourful food!

Ancient Appetites

In ancient China, rice and fish were the staple foods. Fish was sprinkled with ginger to keep it from smelling. Soybeans and tofu were also popular. Poor people lived on rice, cabbage and curd made from soybeans. The wealthy Chinese ate all kinds of expensive food – pork, lamb, duck, goat and fish. They were even known to eat the meat of snakes, dogs, snails and birds! People in ancient China also mixed flavours, chilli peppers, vinegar and pickles in their food to spice it up. Almost every meal was accompanied by tea. People also drank rice wine, fruit juice, honey juice and coconut milk.

Cuisine & Customs

The ancient Chinese had many customs attached to food and dining. Women had to wait for the men to finish their meal before they could eat. The Chinese also believed that food should be eaten with the right hand, as the left hand was considered unclean.

The ancient Chinese custom of eating with chopsticks is followed all over the world today.

Ancient Chinese apothecaries developed cures for aches, pains and fevers by grinding the bones of animals

 What kind of medicines did chemists in ancient China prepare?

It is believed that the ancient Chinese apothecaries (chemists) used the bones, teeth and horns of dragons and other animals to make medicines. Dragon parts were thought to cure nearly all diseases of the human body. The apothecaries would grind these ingredients in machines with their feet and make pills or potions out of them.

Did people in ancient China apply make-up?

Ancient Chinese men and women applied rice powder on their face and coloured their lips and cheeks. They even tweezed their eyebrows to shape them into sharp arches (fashionable during the Han dynasty) or curves.

The ancient Chinese dressed according to their social status

What kind of clothes did the ancient Chinese wear?

People in ancient China dressed according to their wealth. Rich men and women wore heavy silk robes that were decorated with intricate embroidery. Their footwear was made of silk or leather. Poor people wore loose trousers and tunics and sandals made of straw or wood. Their clothes, however, were also embroidered, as this was seen to protect them from evil spirits.

When did tea-drinking become a part of Chinese social customs?

Tea was first drunk in China as a medicine for digestion. It was only in the eighth century that tea became a part of Chinese social customs and events.

FACT BOX

The ancient Chinese added petals of flowers like jasmine in their tea to flavour it

Did people in ancient China practice aromatherapy?

As early as 2700 B.C., aromatherapy was practiced in ancient China. Ancient Chinese medical books that were discovered later list several cures using more than 300 aromatic herbs.

Why were little boys in ancient China made to wear pink and red clothes?

Young boys in ancient China commonly wore pink and red clothes, as these colours were believed to be lucky. The ancient Chinese considered boys to be special and important and hence, wanted to protect them from harm.

How did the ancient Chinese interpret the Big Dipper star pattern?

In ancient China, the star pattern known as the Big Dipper was thought of as a special chariot for the emperor of the heavens!

■ In ancient China, criminals who attacked foreigners or travellers were punished by having their noses or ears cut off!

■ Legend has it that people in ancient China committed suicide by eating a pound of salt.

■ The ancient Chinese are believed to have invented coins. Their coins had a hole in the middle. There were no banks at the time, so people ran strings through these holes to keep their coins safe! In fact, it is said that one thousand strung coins were known as a 'string of money'.

Unusual banking system: the ancient Chinese knew how to keep their money safe!

FASCINATING FACTS

Why were musical gongs used on boats and ships in ancient China?

Gongs were used by water vessels to signal one another about their presence. A special gong player would sit alongside the instrument to perform this duty.

For the ancient Chinese, eating coriander and peaches was the key to living forever

Why did Emperor Shi Huangdi burn the writings of Confucius?

Emperor Shi Huangdi ordered the writings of Confucius to be burnt during his reign. He did so because he wanted to destroy all traces of teachings that he did not agree with. This was one of the earliest attempts at censorship.

The historic book-burning ritual was performed by the dictator Shi Huangdi to destroy anything that could threaten his power

Why were coriander leaves and peaches special to the ancient Chinese?

People in ancient China believed that eating coriander and peaches would make a person immortal!

What is the Red Thread of Destiny?

According to an ancient Chinese belief, people who are fated to be together are connected from birth with an invisible red thread. The Chinese believed that eventually this thread would get smaller and smaller, until the two people connected to it would meet.

What did the ancient Chinese think about bald people?

It is said that baldness in ancient China was seen as a punishment from the devil and was regarded as an infectious disease!

INVENTIONS AND DISCOVERIES

Some of the most important inventions known to man originated in ancient China. From food and drink to technological tools and toys, the Chinese created many of the basic objects we use today.

Printing Pioneers

If it were not for the Chinese, the printing press may not have been known to the world. The first process of printing was invented during the Tang Dynasty. Blocks of wood were used to print religious texts on cloth scrolls. Later, books were printed using the same method. The first known printed book is said to be on the Buddhist religion. Printed in 868 A.D., it was found at the Dunhuang Caves, along the Silk Road in China. Since block-printing was expensive, movable type printing, which was cheaper and faster, was developed in the 11th century. In this method, single Chinese characters were etched on separate blocks of clay.

Diverse Discoveries

The ancient Chinese made ground-breaking discoveries in the fields of mathematics, astrology, astronomy and medicine.

The ancient Chinese were pioneers in printing technology and book production

41

Who discovered tea?

Legend has it that tea was discovered by an ancient Chinese emperor named Shen Nung, around 5000 years ago. According to the story, Shen Nung accidentally discovered tea when some tea leaves from a tree fell into his cup of boiling water. Shen Nung, also called 'The Divine Healer', is believed to have founded herbal medicine.

This unusual earthquake-detector invented in ancient China dropped a ball in the direction of the earthquake

Which ancient Chinese invention helped people to detect earthquakes?

In the second century A.D., the Chinese scientist Chang Heng developed the world's first seismoscope – a device for measuring earthquakes. His invention was a cylinder-shaped container with eight dragon heads around its rim. Each head contained a ball in its mouth. At the bottom were sculptures of frogs with open mouths. In the case of an earthquake, a ball dropped from the dragon's mouth to the frog's mouth and the resulting sound informed people of the earthquake!

Which ancient Chinese invention was useful for labourers and farmers?

Labourers and farmers in ancient China used yokes to carry loads. Yokes were made up of buckets or containers attached to the ends of a stick. These containers were filled with goods. The stick was then placed across the shoulders and carried from place to place.

The ancient Chinese yoke is used by people in China even today

Was the magnetic compass invented in ancient China?

The magnetic compass was invented during the Han Dynasty in ancient China and comprised two parts. The first was a rectangular table was marked with symbols of constellations and directions. The compass needle was in the form of a spoon and it pointed to the south when placed on the table. The table symbolised Earth and the spoon represented Heaven. When the two were joined, they were thought to guide people in the right direction.

The ancient Chinese invented the magnetic compass and used it to travel by sea

Were noodles invented in ancient China?

Noodles were invented in ancient China nearly 2000 years ago. Marco Polo, the famous explorer, is said to have brought noodles from China to Italy, where spaghetti was made soon after.

Who invented paper money?

The ancient Chinese invented paper money around 1000 years ago. They called it 'flying money' as it was light enough to blow out of the hand! The notes were given specific values that were guaranteed by the Chinese government.

Which kind of dessert originated in ancient China?

Ice cream was invented in China in about 200 B.C.! It is believed that a soft mixture of milk and rice was packed in snow and hardened.

FACT BOX

■ The first matchsticks were made in ancient China, around the sixth century A.D. They were made of pinewood and sulphur.

■ Sometime during the seventh century A.D., the ancient Chinese discovered brandy and whisky!

■ Firecrackers were invented in ancient China. The first firecrackers were in fact, dry bamboo sticks that were burnt to produce the sound of crackers. Later, the Chinese developed gunpowder and used it to make firecrackers.

'Pao chuk', the Chinese name for firecrackers means 'burst bamboo'!

INVENTIONS AND DISCOVERIES

❓ Is it true that the first practical umbrella originated in ancient China?

It is believed that the first real umbrella was invented during the Wei Dynasty (386-532 A.D.). This was made out of oil paper, produced from the bark of the mulberry tree. These umbrellas protected against both the rain and the sun. Later, umbrellas were used as status symbols. Royal people carried red and yellow umbrellas, common people had blue ones.

The frames of ancient Chinese umbrellas were made of bamboo

❓ What is acupuncture?

Acupuncture is a system of healing that was invented in ancient China in about 2700 B.C. Acupuncture uses thin needles to pierce a person's body to cure diseases. This method of healing was believed to open up blocked passages of energy in the body and relieve pain.

❓ Did the ancient Chinese make paper?

The process of paper-making is said to have originated in ancient China. Although the Egyptians invented the first form of paper, it was the Chinese who developed paper as we know it today.

❓ How did the ancient Chinese discover silk?

According to legend, silk was discovered by the Chinese princess, Xi Liu Shi, around 2640 B.C. It is said that while she was drinking tea under a mulberry tree, a silk cocoon accidentally fell into her cup. As the cocoon slowly opened up inside the cup, the princess discovered that it consisted of a single thread of silk.

❓ What form of transport did the ancient Chinese invent?

The one-wheeled barrow was invented during the Han Dynasty.
It comprised one huge wheel that supported a flat wooden surface. The barrow was used by gardeners and farmers for

The wheelbarrow in ancient China was also used to transport wounded or dead soldiers from the battlefield